Biodiversity

of Coral Reefs

GREG PYERS

Marshall Cavendish
Benchmark
New York

Library of Congress Cataloging-in-Publication Data

Pyers, Greg.
   Biodiversity of coral reefs / Greg Pyers.
      p. cm. — (Biodiversity)
   Includes index.
   Summary: "Discusses the variety of living things in a coral reef's ecosystem"—Provided by publisher.
   ISBN 978-1-60870-070-7
   1. Coral reef organisms—Juvenile literature. 2. Coral reef ecology—Juvenile literature.
   3. Endangered ecosystems—Juvenile literature. I. Title.
   QH95.8.P94 2010
577.7'89—dc22
                                                        2009042312

First published in 2010 by
MACMILLAN EDUCATION AUSTRALIA PTY LTD
15–19 Claremont Street, South Yarra 3141

Visit our website at www.macmillan.com.au or go directly to www.macmillanlibrary.com.au

Associated companies and representatives throughout the world.

Copyright © Greg Pyers 2010

Edited by Georgina Garner
Text and cover design by Kerri Wilson
Page layout by Kerri Wilson
Photo research by Legend Images
Illustrations by Richard Morden

Printed in China

Acknowledgments
The author and the publisher are grateful to the following for permission to reproduce copyright material:

Front cover photograph of an underwater view of coral and fish courtesy of Digital Vision.
Back cover photograph of a green sea turtle © Lawrence Cruciana/Shutterstock.

Photographs courtesy of:
© Mark Spencer/AUSCAPE, **11**; Brand X Pictures, **7**; Digital Vision, **1**; © Debra Law/Dreamstime.com, **26**; Great Barrier Reef Marine Park Authority, photo by A. Elliott, **27**, photo by J. Jones, **22**, **29**; © 2008 Jupiterimages Corporation, **18**; Photolibrary/ Wolfgang Poelzer, **25**; Photolibrary/Gaffney Rick, **17**; Photolibrary/Science Photo Library, **23**; Photolibrary/Alexis Rosenfeld/SPL, **24**; © Mircea Bezergheanu/Shutterstock, **10**; © Rich Carey/Shutterstock, **4**; © Susan Harris/Shutterstock, **19**; © Noel Powell, Schaumburg/Shutterstock, **21**; © Christophe Testi/Shutterstock, **20**; © Bershadsky Yuri/Shutterstock, **16**.

While every care has been taken to trace and acknowledge copyright, the publisher tenders their apologies for any accidental infringement where copyright has proved untraceable. Where the attempt has been unsuccessful, the publisher welcomes information that would redress the situation.

1 3 5 6 4 2

Contents

Glossary Words

When a word is printed in **bold**, you can look up its meaning in the Glossary on page 31.

What Is Biodiversity?

Biodiversity, or biological diversity, describes the variety of living things in a particular place, in a particular **ecosystem**, or across the entire Earth.

Measuring Biodiversity

The biodiversity of a particular area is measured on three levels:

- **species** diversity, which is the number and variety of species in the area.
- genetic diversity, which is the variety of **genes** each species has. Genes determine the characteristics of different living things. A variety of genes within a species enables it to **adapt** to changes in its environment.
- ecosystem diversity, which is the variety of **habitats** in the area. A diverse ecosystem has many habitats within it.

Species Diversity

Some habitats, such as coral reefs and rain forests, have very high species diversity. One scientific study found 534 species in just 54 square feet (5 square meters) of coral reef in the Caribbean Sea. In the Amazon Rain Forest, in South America, fifty species of ants and many other species were found in just 11 square feet (1 square meter) of leaf litter. In desert habitats, the same area might be home to as few as ten species.

Habitats and Ecosystems

Coral reefs are habitats, which are places where animals and plants live. Within a coral reef habitat, there are also many different types of smaller habitats, sometimes called microhabitats. Some coral reef microhabitats are caves, sandy seabeds, and rocky crevices. Different kinds of **organisms** live in these places. The animals, plants, other living things, nonliving things, and all the ways they affect each other make up a coral reef ecosystem.

Coral reefs are biodiverse. They are home to species of fish, other marine animals, and coral.

Biodiversity Under Threat

The variety of species on Earth is under threat. There are somewhere between 5 million and 30 million species on Earth. Most of these species are very small and hard to find, so only about 1.75 million have been described and named. These are called known species.

Scientists estimate that as many as fifty species become **extinct** every day. Extinction is a natural process, but human activities have sped up the rate of extinction by nearly one thousand times.

Known Species of Organisms on Earth

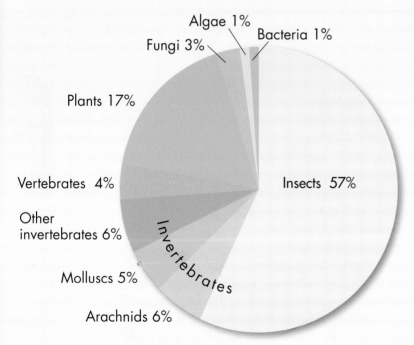

Algae 1%
Bacteria 1%
Fungi 3%
Plants 17%
Vertebrates 4%
Other invertebrates 6%
Molluscs 5%
Arachnids 6%
Insects 57%
Invertebrates

The known species of organisms on Earth can be divided into bacteria, algae, fungi, plant, and animal species. Animal species are further divided into vertebrates and invertebrates.

Approximate Numbers of Known Vertebrate Species

ANIMAL GROUP	KNOWN SPECIES
Fish	31,000
Birds	10,000
Reptiles	8,800
Amphibians	6,500
Mammals	5,500

Why Is Biodiversity Important?

Biodiversity is important for many reasons. The diverse organisms in an ecosystem take part in natural processes essential to the survival of all living things. Biodiversity produces food and medicine. It is also important to people's quality of life.

Natural Processes

Humans are part of many ecosystems. Our survival depends on the natural processes that go on in these ecosystems. Through natural processes, air and water are cleaned, waste is decomposed, **nutrients** are recycled, and disease is kept under control. Natural processes depend on the organisms that live in the soil, on the plants that produce oxygen and absorb **carbon dioxide**, and on the organisms that break down dead plants and animals. When species of organisms become extinct, natural processes may stop working.

Food

We depend on biodiversity for our food. The world's major food plants are grains, vegetables, and fruits. These plants have all been bred from plants in the wild. Wild plants are important sources of genes for breeding new disease-resistant crops. If these wild plants were to become extinct, their genes would be lost.

Medicine

About 40 percent of all prescription drugs come from chemicals that have been extracted from plants. Scientists discover new, useful plant chemicals every year. The National Cancer Institute discovered that 70 percent of plants found to have anticancer properties were rain forest plants.

When plant species become extinct, the chemicals within them are lost forever. The lost chemicals might have been important in making new medicines.

Did You Know?

Biodiversity varies over time. Fossils show us that many species of animals and plants that lived in coral reefs in the past have since become extinct.

Quality of Life

Biodiversity is important to our quality of life. Animals and plants inspire wonder. They are part of our **heritage**. Some species have become particularly important to us. If the Asian elephant became extinct, our survival would not be affected, but we would feel great sadness and regret.

Extinct Species

The dodo was a large, flightless bird that lived on the island of Mauritius, in the Indian Ocean. The first people to see the dodo were European sailors in the 1500s. Sailors hunted the dodo for its meat. They also introduced monkeys and pigs onto the island. These animals ate the dodos' eggs and nestlings. By 1681 the dodo was extinct. Since then, the dodo has become a symbol of extinction.

Great plant biodiversity produces a great variety of fruits and vegetables.

Coral Reefs of the World

A coral reef is a structure made by plantlike animals called **polyps**. Coral reefs are found in warm, shallow waters. The total area of coral reefs in the world today is 109,800 square miles (284,300 square kilometers), an area about half the size of France.

Where Coral Reefs Are Found

Coral reefs form in warm, shallow seas. Most of the world's coral reefs are found in **tropical** areas and along coasts, where water depth is 130 feet (40 m) or less. Some coral reefs are found in **temperate** areas.

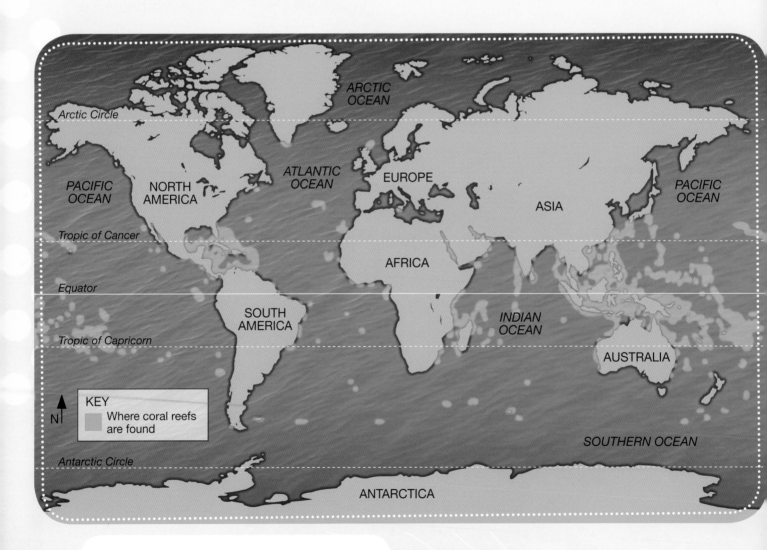

ARCTIC OCEAN

Arctic Circle

PACIFIC OCEAN

NORTH AMERICA

ATLANTIC OCEAN

EUROPE

ASIA

PACIFIC OCEAN

Tropic of Cancer

AFRICA

Equator

SOUTH AMERICA

INDIAN OCEAN

Tropic of Capricorn

AUSTRALIA

N

KEY
Where coral reefs are found

SOUTHERN OCEAN

Antarctic Circle

ANTARCTICA

Most coral reefs are found in the tropics, which is the area between the Tropic of Cancer and the Tropic of Capricorn.

Which Countries Have Coral Reefs?

There are eighty countries and geographical locations with coral reefs. The table below shows the twenty countries with the largest areas of coral reef.

Countries With the Largest Areas of Coral Reef		
COUNTRY	CORAL REEF AREA (square miles)	PERCENTAGE OF WORLD TOTAL
Indonesia	19,700	17.9
Australia	18,900	17.2
Philippines	9,680	8.8
France, including Clipperton Island, Mayotte, Réunion, Guadeloupe, Martinique, New Caledonia, French Polynesia, and Wallis and Futuna Islands	5,510	5.0
Papua New Guinea	5,340	4.9
Fiji	3,870	3.5
Maldives	3,440	3.1
Saudi Arabia	2,570	2.3
Marshall Islands	2,360	2.1
India	2,240	2.0
Solomon Islands	2,220	2.0
United Kingdom, including British Indian Ocean Territory, Anguilla, Bermuda, Cayman Islands, Pitcairn Islands, Turks and Caicos Islands, and the British Virgin Islands	2,130	1.9
Federated States of Micronesia	1,680	1.5
Vanuatu	1,590	1.4
Egypt	1,470	1.3
United States of America, including Hawaii, American Samoa, Puerto Rico, U.S. Virgin Islands, and Guam	1,460	1.3
Malaysia	1,390	1.3
Tanzania	1,380	1.3
Eritrea	1,260	1.1
Bahamas	1,220	1.1

Coral Reef Biodiversity

Coral reefs are the habitats of many **marine** species, including the tiny polyps that form the coral. They are places of high biodiversity. More species live in coral reefs than in any other part of the sea.

Many brightly colored fish species live in tropical reef habitats.

How Coral Reefs Form

A coral reef forms over thousands of years. The structure of the reef is formed by tiny plantlike animals, called polyps. Each polyp uses salts from the sea water to build a cuplike limestone skeleton around itself. This is called coral. Millions of polyps produce so much coral that a reef is formed. This provides a habitat for many other marine species.

High Biodiversity

Coral reefs have very high biodiversity. Coral reefs take up less than 0.25 percent of the ocean floor, but they are the habitat of 25 percent of marine fish species. More than 4,000 species of fish have been identified in coral reefs and there are many more yet to be discovered.

Coral reefs have high biodiversity because they have many habitats within them. They are also many thousands of years old, so species are adapted to living in these habitats. Species thrive in the warm temperature of the waters where tropical coral reefs form.

Differences in Coral Reefs

All coral reefs have high biodiversity, but their biodiversity levels vary from one part of the world to another. Coral reefs with the greatest biodiversity are found around the Philippines. In these reefs, there are more than 400 species of coral. In the Great Barrier Reef, off the coast of Australia, there are 350 species of coral. The coral reefs of Fiji have 250 species of coral, and the reefs of Hawaii have fewer than 50 species.

Endemic Species

Many coral reef species are found in different coral reefs around the world, but some coral reefs also have **endemic species**. The coral reefs of the Red Sea have a very high number of endemic species. If the Red Sea reefs were to disappear, these species would become extinct.

Many different species of coral live together in the one habitat.

Fish Species Diversity

In the Philippines, more than 2,000 species of fish live on or near coral reefs. The coral reefs around Hawaii have about 450 species of fish, the Great Barrier Reef in Australia has 1,500 species, and the reefs of the Bahamas, in the Caribbean Sea, have about 510 species.

Coral Reef Ecosystems

Living and nonliving things, and the **interactions** between them, make up coral reef ecosystems. Living things are plants and animals. Nonliving things are the rocks, coral structure, sand and water, as well as the **climate**, temperature, and ocean currents.

Food Chains and Food Webs

A very important way that different species interact is by eating or consuming other species. This transfers energy and nutrients from one organism to another. A food chain illustrates this flow of energy, by showing what eats what. A food web shows how many different food chains fit together.

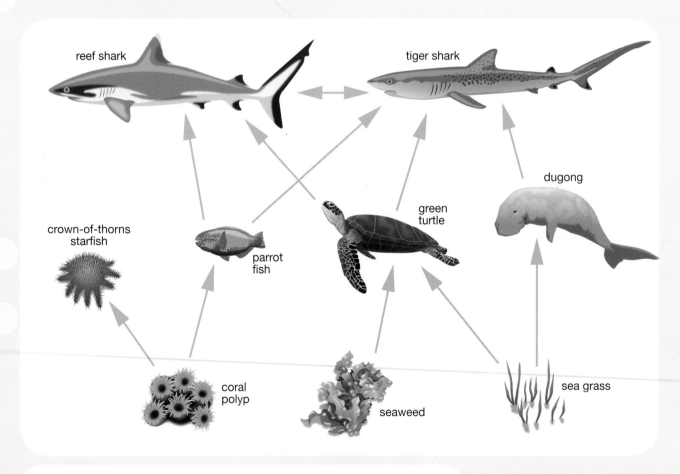

This coral reef food web is made up of several food chains. In one food chain, seaweed is eaten by green turtles, which in turn are eaten by tiger sharks.

Other Interactions

Living things in a coral reef interact in other ways, too. Clown fish are able to live safe from **predators** among the stinging tentacles of another animal, the anemone. The anemone benefits from this relationship by feeding on scraps of food dropped by the clown fish.

Forming Coral

Coral reefs are made by a plant and an animal working together. The animal is called a polyp and it has a plant, called an **alga**, living inside it. The alga makes sugars and oxygen from sunlight, in a process called **photosynthesis**. The polyp uses the sugars and oxygen to grow, and it makes limestone from salts in the sea water. Limestone is what coral is made of. The alga, called zooanthella, stays safe inside the polyp and uses the polyp's wastes to grow.

Coral forms only in shallow water, because zooanthellae need sunlight to produce sugars. Coral is found only in seawater because its limestone is made from dissolved salts found in seawater.

A coral polyp is protected by its outer limestone skeleton. Its tentacles draw in food, which passes down to the mouth and into the stomach.

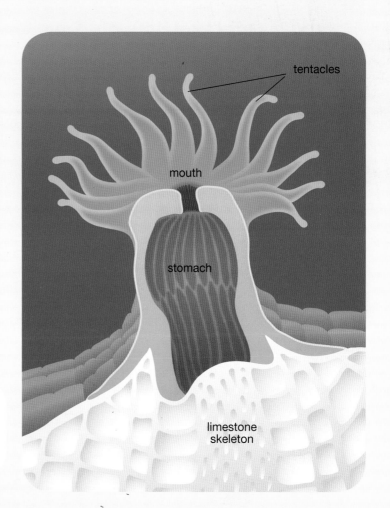

tentacles

mouth

stomach

limestone skeleton

Threats to Coral Reef Biodiversity

Coral reefs around the world are under threat from a range of human activities. The high biodiversity of coral reefs means that the survival of many marine species is in jeopardy.

Biodiversity Hotspots

In 2002, scientists listed ten coral reef areas as biodiversity hotspots. These are regions that have very high biodiversity and that are under severe threat from humans. These ten coral reef hotspots cover only 0.017 percent of the ocean floor, but many of the species that live in them are endemic species. If these areas are not protected, many species will face extinction.

The Ten Coral Reef Hotspots, From Most to Least Threatened

HOTSPOT	HOTSPOT AREA (square miles)	DESCRIPTION
Philippines	8,500	Many small reefs spread over a wide area
Gulf of Guinea	80	Reefs around the Gulf of Guinea islands of Annobón, Bioco, São Tomé, and Príncipe, off western Africa
Sunda Islands	4,900	Reefs around the Sunda Islands, including the islands of Borneo and Sumatra
Southern Mascarene Islands	400	Reefs surrounding the islands of Réunion, Mauritius, and Rodriguez in the Indian Ocean
Eastern South Africa	80	Reefs near Cape Floristic, South Africa
Northern Indian Ocean	4,000	Includes reefs around the Maldives and Sri Lanka, in the Indian Ocean
Southern Japan, Taiwan, and southern China	1,200	Reefs from Kyushu, Japan, through Taiwan to China
Cape Verde Islands	80	Reefs off the western African coast, in the Atlantic Ocean
Western Caribbean	1,500	Reefs from the Yucatan Peninsula, in Mexico, south to Colombia
Red Sea and Gulf of Aden	1,200	Includes reefs in the Red Sea and the gulfs of Aden, Aqaba, and Suez, in the Middle East

Human Threats

Around 58 percent of the world's coral reefs are reported as threatened by human activities. Each of the ten coral reef biodiversity hotspots is seriously affected by several or all of these human-induced threats:

- tourism and **urban** development
- overfishing
- destructive fishing, such as dynamiting
- land clearing
- coral mining
- climate change, due to human activity
- pollution
- shipping.

Most coral reef biodiversity hotspots are found in the Indian and Pacific oceans.

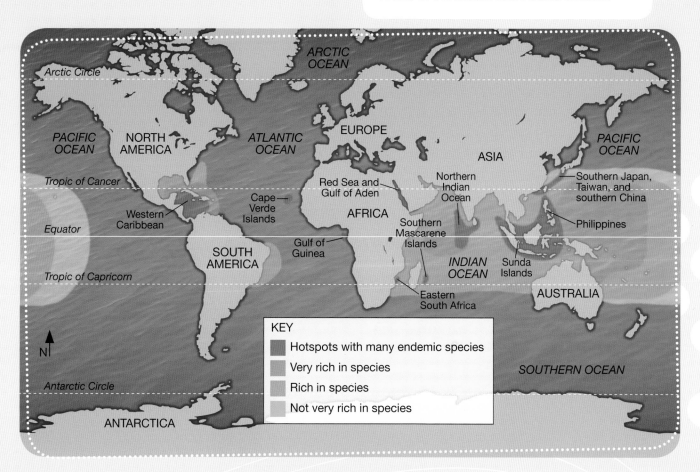

ARCTIC OCEAN

Arctic Circle

PACIFIC OCEAN

NORTH AMERICA

ATLANTIC OCEAN

EUROPE

ASIA

PACIFIC OCEAN

Tropic of Cancer

Red Sea and Gulf of Aden

Northern Indian Ocean

Southern Japan, Taiwan, and southern China

Cape Verde Islands

AFRICA

Western Caribbean

Southern Mascarene Islands

Philippines

Equator

Gulf of Guinea

SOUTH AMERICA

INDIAN OCEAN

Sunda Islands

Tropic of Capricorn

AUSTRALIA

N

Eastern South Africa

SOUTHERN OCEAN

Antarctic Circle

ANTARCTICA

KEY
- Hotspots with many endemic species
- Very rich in species
- Rich in species
- Not very rich in species

15

BIODIVERSITY THREAT:
Fishing

In 2006, a study by the Global Coral Reef Monitoring Network found that the greatest threat to coral reef biodiversity is fishing, both legal and illegal. Some fishing methods destroy the reef environment, and overfishing is threatening reef biodiversity.

Destructive Fishing Methods

Some fishing methods destroy coral reefs. Dynamiting and cyaniding are two fishing methods that are illegal in many countries. Trapping can also damage the reef environment when traps break loose.

Dynamiting

Dynamiting, also called blast fishing, is a very destructive fishing method. A cheap bomb is made using a drink bottle, fertilizer, diesel, and a fuse. The bomb is dropped over the side of a boat. When the bomb explodes, the fish close by are killed. Many dead fish float to the surface where they are collected. More than half the fish, however, sink to the bottom and are not collected. The explosion damages the reef structure.

Cyaniding

In this fishing method, the deadly poison cyanide is injected into reefs where fish hide. The fish become poisoned and are easy to catch. The cyanide is washed from the gills to revive the fish and the captured fish are sold to the aquarium trade. For every fish that is revived, many more die. The cyanide remains in the reef, continuing to kill fish and coral for years to come.

Reef fish are captured and sold to people for their home aquariums.

Did You Know?

Worldwide, there may be 2 million marine aquariums in homes. Most of these aquariums are stocked with fish that were taken from the wild. Many aquarium fish are illegally caught.

Trapping

Fish traps are set on the seafloor. Fish can swim in but cannot swim out. If these traps come loose and drift away, they continue to trap fish. The traps can also break coral or become entangled in it.

Overfishing

Overfishing is when the number of fish taken is so high that fish populations cannot breed fast enough to replenish themselves. Even traditional net fishing can put pressure on fish populations in coral reefs. If there are too many people catching fish, fish numbers decline very quickly and may never recover. Modern commercial fishing causes overfishing if trawlers take too many fish.

Fishing Boat Donations

After the Indian Ocean tsunami of December 26, 2004, charities donated many boats to communities along the affected coastlines. These donations were meant to help local people rebuild their lives. Unfortunately, these donated boats increased the pressure on coral reefs because many more people were able to go fishing in these waters. Along the Tamil Nadu coast of southeastern India, there were 6,500 boats before the 2004 tsunami and 11,000 after the tsunami.

Reef fishing and diving are popular recreational activities, but they can threaten coral reef biodiversity.

BIODIVERSITY THREAT:
Land Clearing and Farming

Coral needs clear water to grow. In murky water, sunlight is blocked out and photosynthesis cannot take place. Seawater becomes murky when land is cleared and soil is washed into the sea. Nutrients and poisons also wash into the sea.

Land Clearing

The clearing of forests and other coastal **vegetation** can affect coral reefs. When coastal vegetation is cleared, the ground becomes exposed to **erosion**. Heavy rains can wash large quantities of soil into rivers, and rivers can carry the soil out to sea as far as 25 miles (40 km).

Most coral reefs are found in shallow water within 25 miles (40 km) of the coast. Soil and sediments carried in the water, called **silt**, settle on the coral and smother it. Siltation is the depositing of silt carried by rivers. If siltation is severe, it can kill coral.

Rivers carry fine soil and sand sediments to the sea.

Drains carry sewage from city streets to the sea. Sewage can harm coral reefs.

Nutrients

Water washed from the land into the sea often carries high levels of nitrogen and phosphorus. Nitrogen and phosphorus come from **sewage** and from fertilizers used on farms. They are nutrients that plants need to grow.

Nitrogen and phosphorus washed into sea water threaten coral reefs because they cause seaweed to grow so thickly that it smothers coral. Phosphorus also causes coral polyps to produce limestone that is less dense than normal, which means the coral that is produced is fragile.

Poisons

Herbicides and pesticides are chemical poisons that are washed into the sea from the land. These chemicals can kill reef fish. Oil washed into the sea from city streets can poison reef animals. It can also damage the feathers of birds that hunt on coral reefs.

Mangroves

Mangroves are trees that grow along the coast. Mangroves absorb large amounts of the nutrients that wash down from the land. When mangrove forests are removed to build roads, marinas, hotels, and ports, more nutrients are able to enter the sea. Algal growth increases and coral growth declines.

BIODIVERSITY THREAT:
Tourism and Shipping

Coral reefs are very popular with tourists, but large numbers of tourists can cause a lot of damage. Another threat to reefs comes from the many ships that pass by coral reefs on their way from port to port.

Tourism

People go to coral reefs to snorkel or scuba dive, or to take trips in glass-bottomed boats to see the colorful corals, fish, and other reef animals. Many people enjoy the warm tropical climate. Tourism provides work for local people and brings money into the local economy.

Pieces of coral and shells are sometimes taken by tourists, destroying the coral habitat.

Damage Caused by Tourism

Tourism may help local communities but it can also damage coral reefs. Tourist boats may damage coral when they drop anchor, and some people break off pieces of coral to take home as souvenirs.

When large numbers of tourists begin visiting an area, hotels and roads are built. This increases the amount of pollution, such as sewage, oil, and plastic, that is washed into the sea from the land. This pollution can kill coral reef organisms.

Coral Disease

Coral disease, caused by bacteria, fungi, and viruses, appears to have increased in the past ten years. Scientists believe corals lose their immunity to these germs when they become stressed by pollution, which is often caused by tourism and shipping.

A shipwreck in the Caribbean Sea is slowly taken over by corals.

Shipping

Ships are a threat to coral reefs. If a ship goes off course, it can run into a reef and destroy large areas of coral. The paint used on ships' hulls has a poison in it called tributyltin (TBT) to keep **barnacles** from attaching themselves to the hulls. If this paint is scraped off when a ship runs into coral, it poisons coral reef animals, including coral polyps. A damaged reef may take many decades to recover.

Oil Spills

With shipping, there is always a risk of oil spills. Oil spills poison marine life and coat the feathers of seabirds so that they are unable to fly.

Shipping Accidents

The first ship to run aground on Australia's Great Barrier Reef was the HMS *Endeavour*, commanded by James Cook, on June 11, 1770. This ship was wooden and damage to the reef was very minor. On November 2, 2000, a container ship called the *Bunga Teratai Satu* ran aground and caused severe damage to the reef, south of the *Endeavour*'s collision site. The ship's owners were fined $325,000 to repair the damage.

BIODIVERSITY THREAT:
Climate Change

The world's average temperature is rising, in a process known as global warming. This warming is causing changes to the world's climate. These climate changes are affecting coral reefs.

Rising Temperatures

The increase in average global temperature is because levels of certain gases, such as carbon dioxide, are increasing in Earth's atmosphere. These gases are called greenhouse gases. They trap heat in the atmosphere, like glass does in a greenhouse. The increase in temperature is causing changes to the climate. Some of these changes affect coral reefs.

Coral Bleaching

Coral bleaching occurs when sea surface temperature rises a few degrees Fahrenheit over a period of a few weeks. When this happens, coral polyps eject the algae that live inside them and the coral turns white. If sea temperatures remain high, the coral can die.

Before 1979, mass coral bleaching had not been recorded. Since then, the frequency of coral bleaching has been increasing. Widespread bleaching has devastated reefs in regions such as the Maldives and the Seychelles islands in the Indian Ocean, and the Pacific island nation of Palau. Scientists predict that coral bleaching may occur every year this century.

When sea surface temperatures rise, coral reefs may turn white and die.

Did You Know?

The highest sea surface temperature increases in history were recorded in 1998. These increases caused 46 percent of all coral reefs in the western Indian Ocean to be damaged or killed by coral bleaching.

Ocean Acidification

When carbon dioxide is dissolved in water, it makes a weak acid called carbonic acid. An increase in carbon dioxide in the atmosphere causes the oceans to become more acidic, as the seawater absorbs more carbon dioxide. This is disastrous for coral reefs because polyps cannot build their limestone skeletons in acidic oceans. Some scientists predict that if carbon dioxide levels do not fall, coral reefs will disappear altogether by the end of this century.

Turtles

Rising temperatures have serious effects on many coral reef animals, such as marine turtles. The temperature of the sand in which eggs are laid determines the sex of the turtles in the eggs. The higher the temperature, the greater the proportion of female turtles that will develop. Global warming would mean fewer males for mating.

Many species lose their habitat when a reef suffers coral bleaching.

23

Coral Reef Conservation

Conservation is the protection, preservation, and wise use of resources. With at least 11 percent of the world's coral reefs destroyed in the past century and up to 80 percent of them overfished, coral reefs need urgent conservation.

The Importance of Reefs

Coral reefs are very important to the many species that live in and around them. They are also very important for people. A healthy coral reef can provide 40 tons (36 tonnes) of seafood per square mile each year. In the Philippines, about 70 percent of a person's animal protein comes from seafood. Indonesia's coral reefs are worth $1.6 billion a year to its economy through fish production and tourism.

Research

Research surveys or studies are used to find out information about coral reefs, such as how coral reef ecosystems work and how humans affect them. Research helps people work out ways to conserve coral reefs. The people who carry out reef research are scientists who work for government departments or for organizations that take responsibility for managing coral reefs.

A research scientist collects coral samples to study.

Sea Star Research

Crown-of-thorns starfish are sea stars that live in coral reefs where they feed on coral polyps. Occasionally, the population of this sea star soars, and eats and destroys large areas of coral. Scientific research has found that fish eat sea star larvae. Overfishing of an area leads to more sea star larvae surviving to adulthood, which leads to these large population increases and reef destruction.

A crown-of-thorns starfish feeds on a coral reef.

Marine Reserves

A very important way of conserving coral reefs is by creating marine reserves. Fishing is banned and fish are able to breed undisturbed in marine reserves. Most of the world's coral reefs, however, are not protected as reserves.

Education

Information should be passed on and people should be educated as to how they can help conserve coral reefs. People who fish on coral reefs should be taught why fishing in marine reserves is not permitted. Owners of tourist boats need to be told about the damage their anchors can do to coral. Once people understand that their own survival depends on healthy coral reefs, they are more likely to work to protect the reefs.

Did You Know?

Creating marine reserves can help rebuild populations of fish. Five years after a series of marine reserves was set up around the Caribbean island of St. Lucia, the number of fish caught in nearby fishing grounds nearly doubled.

CASE STUDY:
The Great Barrier Reef

The Great Barrier Reef is the largest coral reef system in the world. It consists of more than 2,500 individual reefs and it stretches for more than 1,250 miles (2,000 km) along the northeastern coast of Australia. Its total area of coral reef is 7,700 square miles (20,000 sq km).

Biodiversity of the Reef

Like other coral reefs, the Great Barrier Reef in Australia has high biodiversity. It is home to 5,000 species of mollusc, including slugs, octopuses, and squids. It is also home to seventeen species of sea snake, six of the world's seven species of marine turtle, and 1,500 species of sponge. Dugongs and several species of dolphins and whales live along the Great Barrier Reef, and more than 250 bird species nest on its islands.

Did You Know?

The Great Barrier Reef is the largest structure ever built by any organism, including humans.

The Great Barrier Reef is the largest coral reef system on Earth.

Tourists come from all over the world to snorkel at the Great Barrier Reef.

Formation of the Reef

The Great Barrier Reef first formed around 18 million years ago. Sea levels have risen and fallen many times since then. When sea levels fell, the coral died. When they rose again, the coral reformed where the ancient reef had existed before. Today's reef began growing 15,000 years ago, when sea levels rose after the last **ice age**.

People and the Reef

For thousands of years, indigenous Australians lived on islands throughout the reef, along the Queensland coast to its west, and in the Torres Strait Islands to its north. Today, the region is home to more than 1.4 million people and more than 2 million tourists visit the reef each year. Such a large number of people can have a major effect on the health of the Great Barrier Reef.

Fishing on the Great Barrier Reef

Around two hundred charter boats are permitted to take people out to the Great Barrier Reef to fish. Every year, recreational fishers catch 4,400 tons (3,392 t) of reef fish. The total fish catch along the Great Barrier Reef is worth about $150 million a year. This catch includes 11,000 tons (9,980 t) of prawns.

CASE STUDY: The Great Barrier Reef

Protecting the Great Barrier Reef

The Great Barrier Reef is recognized as a World Heritage Site and it is protected under Australian law.

World Heritage Status

The Great Barrier Reef was added to the United Nations Educational, Scientific and Cultural Organization (UNESCO) World Heritage List in 1981. This list includes places of outstanding international importance. World Heritage listing requires a commitment to protect a site from threats. The Great Barrier Reef is protected as a marine park under Australian law.

Management of the Park

The Great Barrier Reef is among the best-protected coral reefs in the world. The entire 135,000 square miles (348,000 sq km) of the Great Barrier Reef World Heritage Site is managed by the Great Barrier Reef Marine Park Authority (GBRMPA) and the Queensland Government.

The GBRMPA has divided the reef into zones. It makes decisions on which activities can take place in different zones. The zones range from general use zones, where activities such as fishing and shipping are allowed, to preservation zones, where no access is permitted at all.

The GBRMPA also has to approve all tourism activities on the reef, from sightseeing flights to the construction of piers for tourist boats. There are heavy fines for people who break the zoning rules, pollute the reef, or break any other regulations.

Did You Know?

Tourism on the Great Barrier Reef is worth about $600 million a year to the Australian economy.

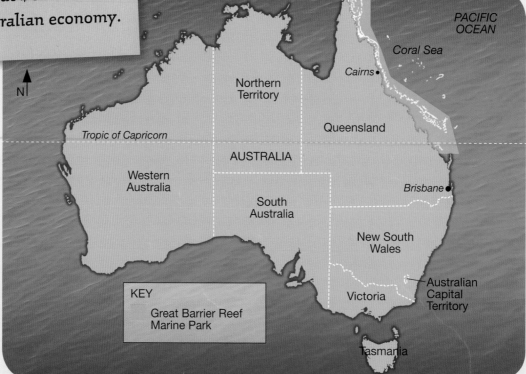

KEY

Great Barrier Reef Marine Park

Research on the Reef

Scientific research is very important for coral reef conservation. The GBRMPA works with universities to study the Great Barrier Reef. It has conducted research studies on turtle and dugong breeding, fish populations, and coral bleaching. By finding out about the coral reef ecosystem and how people affect it, the GBRMPA works out ways to protect the reef and its wildlife.

A researcher takes a blood sample from a green turtle in the Great Barrier Reef Marine Park.

Educating People

Educating tourists and local people about the Great Barrier Reef is an important part of the work of the GBRMPA and the Queensland and Australian governments. The GBRMPA provides information for schools and the public. It educates people about threatened species, climate change, park regulations, and responsible ways to enjoy the reef, such as how to dive and snorkel without damaging coral. It also educates the tourism and fishing industries, such as by teaching operators of prawn fishing boats ways to avoid catching marine turtles in their nets.

What Is the Future of Coral Reefs?

Coral reefs have grown, died, and grown again as sea levels have fallen and risen over millions of years. Today, human activities threaten coral reef biodiversity. When threats are removed, however, this decline can be slowed or even stopped.

What Can You Do For Coral Reefs?

You can help protect coral reefs in many ways:

- Find out about coral reefs. Why are they important and what threatens them?
- If you live near a coast, join a volunteer group that cleans up the beach or replants coastal areas. This will help prevent soil being washed onto the reef.
- When you visit a coral reef, be careful not to walk on the coral and never break off pieces of coral to take as souvenirs.
- Become a responsible consumer. Do not litter and do not buy coral jewelry or reef fish for your aquarium if they may have been collected illegally.
- If you are concerned about environmental problems in your area, or in other areas, send a letter to or e-mail your local newspaper, your state congressperson, or local representative, and express your concerns. Know what you want to say, set out your arguments, be sure of your facts, and ask for a reply.

Useful Websites

💻 **www.reef.edu.au/**
This website has information about how reefs form, reef species, threats to reefs, reef research, and lots of reef facts.

💻 **www.biodiversityhotspots.org**
This website has information about the richest and most threatened areas of biodiversity on Earth.

💻 **www.iucnredlist.org**
The International Union for Conservation of Nature (IUCN) Red List has information about threatened plant and animal species.

Glossary

adapt Change in order to survive.

alga (plural: algae) Simple marine plant without leaves.

barnacles Marine animals that resemble shellfish and grow on rocks, piers, and ship hulls.

carbon dioxide A colorless and odorless gas produced by plants, animals, and the burning of coal and oil.

climate The weather conditions in a certain region over a long period of time.

ecosystem The living and nonliving things in a certain area and the interactions between them.

endemic species Species found only in a particular area.

erosion Wearing away of soil and rock by wind or water.

extinct Having no living members.

genes Segments of deoxyribonucleic acid (DNA) in the cells of a living thing, which determine characteristics.

habitats Places where animals, plants, or other living things live.

heritage Things we inherit and pass on to future generations.

ice age A period of several thousand years in which Earth's temperature was very low and ice sheets covered a large part of Earth.

interactions Actions that are taken together or that affect each other.

marine Of the sea.

nutrients Substances that are used by living things for growth.

organisms Animals, plants, and other living things.

photosynthesis The process by which plants make sugars from carbon dioxide and water, using sunlight for energy.

polyps Small marine animals that make coral.

predators Animals that kill and eat other animals.

sewage Human and animal waste.

silt Fine sand, soil, and other materials carried by water and deposited as sediment.

species A group of animals, plants, or other living things that share the same characteristics and can breed with one another.

temperate In a region or climate that has mild temperatures.

tropical In the hot and humid region between the Tropic of Cancer and the Tropic of Capricorn.

tsunami Long, high sea wave caused by an undersea earthquake.

urban Of towns and cities.

vegetation Plants.

Index